AF342452

SOLI

RAY DIPALMA

an Ithaca House book

Ithaca

Grateful acknowledgement is due the following magazines:

The Little Magazine, The Application, Tottel's, Journal 31, Stooge, Center, The North Stone Review, Hearse, and *Measure.*

Cover photos by Elisabeth Brandfass.

ISBN 0-87886-026-6 (cloth)
ISBN 0-87886-027-4 (paper)

ITHACA HOUSE
108 N. PLAIN STREET
ITHACA, NEW YORK 14850

CONTENTS

SCALES

Crumbling mote one region which jealously reduced
dying to a police presented unrestrained rubbish.
Finally he gets lost in a forest moving himself for-
ward with facial gestures.

Deaf knew altogether I'm in my silence perplexed
tuners being none himself myself dismiss a term
of prevalence a prevalent term. One and the same
thing.

I am naked to its furthest limits as a result. Sustain
its legs however for the little matter of its logical
possibilities.

Though the single event does succeed knowledge
of this arrangement in his room made of according
famished he formulates a series of rearrangements.

It is. It. Is. It is essential to labour the
broken pot. Any term he dismiss apply because what
they really meant his character is shadow. Poetry.

Fairly traditional says morning is refused to
acquiesce and strip denunciation to translation.
Activity manifold but. Keep his activity secured
by religion wisecracks and soda.

The farmers have left for the valley. Back behind
the barn a broken pot and the shack of glory grey
brown green the army.

Who has become this far. Be. Knows me. Come.
Advised by what yesterday's night contained.
The change is impossible.

Assigned duration. The plan. A number of familiar
gaieties. He took her naked by the hairy hand.
Justice huddled. An accumulated name.

Our himself. When jealous is westward. Our herself
is sex. Fleeting into her eastward westward. Cock-
eyed permuter. Both as woman and nothing real
here now but smell.

Two lifelong eternities. In tense the silly present.
Sucking. A clear credit to reality. No one not no
one.

An extravagant anonymity after extravagance. After
extravagance. Who knows what I am more than I am
now—only you and I now. Now.

The new hope of recent months is a matter of baldness.
To forget. He breezed by unconcerned with the headlines.
SEVERAL MENDED CASKETS IN ANTARCTICA. Just like a
hairdresser.

The sound of vicissitude was his saddle. Bring it out
into the public domain and the critics will tell you
where it came from and (as a result) where you can
return it. Poor you.

But today. Today at last. At last. A circle of hair.
One hair in a circle whips my soul like a provincial
Chinese chrysanthemum (1907). O the donkey of the
past is classicism *giddy-yap*!

The lamp of curiosity is. What the eye musters
a bit beyond the feeble flame. All alone and vanishing.
In a discussion of itself sleep was suggested beyond
the pale but crisp hill of the lyric. Wrinkled dream.

Sad among the strangers. Nothing like it. Milk of
the mind. Sad among the strangers, he said. It was
a weapon.

Homage. Mr. Saul Bouquet. Symptom of Pym. As I am.

1968

MERCHARD

A Fragment

Among Merchard's papers......

in my hand
is an island

She disappeared into a bridgeless river. As, Coulez insisted, did her mother, years before. Lucio Coulez, in a confidence to me, stated he had been on certain occasions, privy to many of the bizarre requests Merchard believed she had reason to make as she grew older and, as she strongly felt, less appealing to her sister Nina, twenty years her senior, to the day. Lucio reported that on one occasion Merchard asked that upon her death her entire library, some 12,000 volumes, be destroyed, with the exception of the rare copy of *Theophrastan Characters* which she always kept at her desk. Of its disposal, Merchard said nothing. The respective murder and suicide of Lucio and Nina placed the responsibility of destroying the library in my hands. Today, a week following Lucio's murder, I undertook the task. As Merchard requested, I preserved the copy of *Theophrastan Characters.* On the flyleaf the inscription in Merchard's hand reads......

Among whom to be numbered is knowledge

The book is still in my possession, as well as a scrap of paper containing the words quoted above.

—Lucianino Merchard
Sudrinia, 1837

Bouchardelle
22 February 1837

My Dear Lucianino,

Since Merchard's elegant death your aunt Nina grows in-
creasingly difficult to care for. I had thought these weeks
at Bouchardelle would have settled her mind. But no. She
wanders about the orchards at all hours fingering her beads
like a mad woman. I even begin to question my own san-
ity. She asks incessantly that I speak of my relationship
with Merchard. As Merchard's private secretary over a
twenty year period I came to know many things that I
realize Merchard, in spite of her love for Nina, could never
have spoken of to anyone save me. You are young, but
must understand that such knowledge is a great burden to
a man of my breeding and temperament. I loved Merchard
as only such a man can love. But Nina grows more distrac-
ted and cruel each day. As the rain makes a return to Su-
drinia impossible at this time, I am posting along with this
letter a number of fragments discovered on the first day of
our arrival at Bouchardelle. As you can see the pages were
first crumpled then carefully reopened and folded. Appa-
rently Merchard had second thoughts about destroying these
moments. I found them (oddly enough) at the bottom of
her sewing basket. At first I had decided I would show them
to Nina, but as she became moody and started almost im-
mediately to question me about Merchard, I decided against
it. Please extend my regards to Fra Dominico at the Biblio-
teca San Marcello. You may wish to pass on these fragments
to him. But, then again, if I know you as I think, you may
not. Please accept my apologies for the graceless phrasing of
this brief. Evidence of what these weeks with Nina have
done to me. I feel I must say this, I cannot be responsible.

Affectionately,

Lucio Coulez

The pages of fragments that follow were written by Merchard
most probably during her last stay at the Chateau Bouchar-
delle in November, 1836. It was her custom to jot down
notes and images as they came to her throughout the day.
Only when she felt moved to do so would she begin to order
the pieces into a finished work.

—Fra Dominico Giordano
Biblioteca San Marcello
Sudrinia, 1837

Between the silence

safety

a resilience due

And the method
the method of safety

fails

------

the wind falling from
previous messages

Safety
Adam said
later
by way of

was a resilience due.

Later

a condition of time
by way of

My age contained
In the time of day

In a city large
or small

      crowned in a new room
      the colour of her face

      the nuance   her legs
      her hair

____

I am cold in the day's warmth

     it swallows
   the slippery plummet

 I expected little more

to compose long sentences for your name
     written in the stillness
     of another's eyes

____

a question of choice

who brought us
fire on the iceberg,

shall I.

   The human beauty
     is in the longing

   head.

language goes on in the history of
its references

occasionally references stop
        we have meaning. Attacks

life death

   and the implied discrepancies

(anything meaningful)

      red & green

What is mine. What is still Merchard's. I know (better than
most, who expect the answers now) this is no place to
speak of the beauty that was Merchard's. I write of *place* as
a state of mind—a condition of time. Time with its cross-
weavings that hold all the answers too intricate to unfold.
Amazing intricacies when considered made by those as
gross as fools. I state what I am. I deny myself passively
for what is mine is still Merchard's. I took her for my mo-
ther without ever suspecting that she was. All other answers
are to be doubted. The strange truth (that must not be
strange) lies between need and appetite. I would have more
silence.

—Lucianino Merchard
Sudrinia, 1837

Biblioteca San Marcello
3 March 1837

My Dearest Lucio,

Our young Hamlet, Lucianino, came to me this evening
with the poem fragments of Merchard which you dis-
covered at Bouchardelle. I must say I was quite astoun-
ded that he would entrust them to me. As he said little,
I thought it best not to question him as to his reason
for doing so. However, he did remind me of Merchard's
request concerning the destruction of her library. There
are many rare volumes in her collection, my dear Lucio.
And you know as well as I that these books should find
their place in the Biblioteca San Marcello and not be
disposed of in the mad way she demanded. But of course
my hands are tied. In late January I went to speak to
Lucianino about this matter; he refused to see me. And
now he brings me three pages in Merchard's own hand
for safekeeping. He is perversely unpredictable. I ga-
thered from what little he said that Nina has you in quite
a state. Unless you can advise a better alternative I sug-
gest that you gather your senses together enough to write
Lucianino about saving these books. I think it best that
I refrain from speaking to him of this matter altogether.
In the meantime I shall make copies of the fragments and
send them to Merchard's old confessor Padre Cantarillo
at the Monastery San Sebastian. These fragments are
among the most arcane of any of Merchard's work I have
yet seen. Perhaps the old fool can make something of
them. The original pages I will place in the vault, of
course. Cantarillo's leaving the Biblioteca upon Merchard's
death surprised very few and me least of all. I know that
you are in the midst of the rainy season at Bouchardelle
and am looking forward to your return to Sudrinia. A

17

shipment of Burgundy has arrived for the monks at
the Biblioteca as a gift from the Tambellini estate. Un-
til we may share a bit of it, I send my love and bene-
diction. Above all take care that you write Lucianino
concerning Merchard's volumes.

In Christo,

Fra Dominico Giordano

COLOGNE

The paintbrush smothered the slowly ascending scream

The Steubenville profit has a medium size pulpit

The excavations of last December turned purple

The floating accommodations were signed by public citizens

The laughter rests in your hands tomorrow

The Memorial Seams shouldn't be pursued without police

The turnpike necks are undreamt of

The little fool starched the charms with Connecticut dispensers

The stone or apple hit the deer

The chalet by your trousers is owned by American Express

The fractured wings shook loose the fireweed

The left hand is best considered so

The pile of brick dust has a boggy resonance

The pooch loves snow when its catty-corner to a briquette

The past failures and successes sound like needles

The girl from California has long legs

The portulacas are in a boisterous muddle

The carpenter has a brother named Eric

The porcelain china on the wet steps is wet

The blouse in the corridor was kissed

The lieutenant broke the shutters and let in the darkness

The chef at Tivoli's ate a tomato sandwich with poor posture

The bird swooped like an airplane lands to avoid birds

The Chinaman put his hand in your mouth

The crotchety farmer cemented his tree

The lapels avoided criticism

The young communist brought a great sense of relief

The alarm clock abandoned the coast

The sewer was subjunctive

The closed door opened

The planet Mildred exposed a crushed snail

The helicopters canvassed the aluminum funeral

The mouth sometimes provides a regular routine

The finish line was invited to dine with high society

The more interesting bread was falsified and intolerant

The clerk gathered speed on Tuesday

The belly conferred with the encyclopedia

The fenders turned tail and flipped through a pamphlet

The patrol glanced at his humility

The antennae were half-way up the Madam

The charities pinballed in the nude

The skate key is in the creme de menthe from Paula

The lounge died of thirst

The creature on your hip has a job in Wisconsin

The funnel went to Pittsburgh for surgery

The Cheese Anthology won't fit in your watch band

The smoker broke his wrist

The grass was illuminated by three old fireflies

The parrot who sells newspapers now shines shoes

The Denver sheets were brought to Alfred the Drudge

The comma is bent on suicide

The calendar lurks

The photo of Proust you gave me is now 63 years old

The phalanx is sold on theology

The symbols for cabana and bully are beach ball and beach

The bleeding handles were excused from tarnish school

The vestigial spittle had creased the cows

The dinky twitch you called rhythm fenced the butterscotch

The disguised oversimplifications were sort of funny

The brass breast was a partial failure

The rug fell asleep over natural history

The commandos have money worries with Veronica

The Sanhedrin cooked an apple stew for Bruce

The bald girl held my hand

The piss ant tickled the barnacle

The Sadduccees were hardassed but easily committed
                              to memory

The third lady from the left has been known to limp

The castanets were holding down the fort

The senator was tempted

The drunk, for example, said the bulletins were a commercial hit

The revolver even went to the birthday party in Maine

The decline of Christmas as a banana is very good

The curtain choked the pellet

The Elizabethans rarely went to the jungle

The prairie schooner is damp

The jolly duck shot the ostrich and the kangaroo

The vicious attack progressed handsomely

The luncheonette was crowded with Serbians

The sleeper scratched the thunder

The extenuating pillars were late for the drumroll

The seeds will guffaw the ambulance

The tropical deltas are without valentines

The more aggressive infatuations get a trowel

The appetitie sparkled with information concerning the sky and lakes

The new window won't change your memory

HORNER

Horner
used a short needle
for loving—
he knew what he was
talking about.

A short boy—
dirty all his life.
Uncle ran a store—
ran to fires
when he heard the
sirens go. . .

When I told him
this tie I had
belonged to an Iowa
hangin' judge,
he said,
"I got an answer for that."
And grew silent.

A shot glass
at the mirror
dispersed the sentiment.

I walked across the room
and shut my mouth.

No gun—
and his hair
was thinning. When
he drank he never
took time to swallow.

*   *   *

Sam Bitterice
said his name
like he wasn't sure

it fit—
        Horner and
Sam's nephew
robbed him first.

Then Nephew suggested
they move to the woods.

A pervert observed!—

Horner shot him in the back.

Distortion . . . That's it!
he whispered.
Nephew never had the gallant kind.

His teeth
held a cigarette.

That weekend
in the country
nearly scuffed
his escape.

*   *   *

Horner pulled up
at the Hotel Ceaseless—
still going—
his car and the hotel
both.

"A room with a view,"
says H,
"And put my bed near
a bottle of what
I never swallow.

Where's Jane?"

"Out back
fucking Karl . . . ?"
ventured Clerk.

Horner rubbed
his chest
for iron.

"Karl's
dead, you pocky
cunt! Lou back
from the river
already?"

Clerk
adjusted his ink.
Horner smashed his face.

'I said
IS LOU DROWNED!?"

Clerk nodded
and passed key # 26
to Horner.

"I'll let you live
and make a pretense
out of being friendly.
26's my favorite
so send them up
when they finish out back.

WITH THE BOTTLE!"

Horner's shadow
kites
up the stairs
to # 26

The bottle
was waiting.

It found the street.

"NOT NOW!"
Horner mentions
to the floor.

"Clerk! Your face's
next on the clock!"

Silence whimpered
as he pissed
in the sink.

     *   *   *

After Bitterice
Cabby Luke
found a hole in his
head, it was
Luke's Chequered
got Horner
to the hotel.

Between Bitterice
and Luke
marched twelve shadows
Horner rendered
articulate
of what we only
look for . . .
While words
turn green
in our head.

But the syringe
let him hold
his asshole
in his arms.

The strap
creaked
loose
as he fell back
across the bed.

Nephew's ghost
chewed its ears.
Cabby Luke
dreamed amber
in Horner's
unique blindness.
Bitterice survived
the lenient snarls
this dose
conjured.

A bright fade.

Knock.

Death defeats all signatures,
mumbled H.

Jane touched his mouth.

Lou
winked back
a fart.

A mirrorful of birds
rehearsed him into
Jane's arms. Awake and a
sniff of Lou.

"Jane . . . Lou . . ."
his tongue
followed the light.

"Jane! that SUGAR
makes me gasp.

"Lou! You still
swimming?
                I want
what's left
of out back!"

Horner grabbed
her cunt
and Jane
bruised no destiny
with innocence
as Lou
left by the window.

She lifted her
leg and rolled.

Horner came off
like a lit
cigarette
dropped
from a speeding
car . . . .

1969

WEDNESDAY OR THURSDAY

Bothering fix = mathematics

*

50 years old
    in the knees

*

on the beam- frivolous

*

The Green Prize

        1) foams
        2) is destroyed
            a) by fire
            b) teeth
        3) gets short (perfect)

*

No, I am not up
        for the dance.

Darkness? No, I have no
            preference.

*

I must cover
    what I can
    You can
cover what you
        like

*

In bed
she turns

with
gay suspicion

*

an explanation dawns on me

*

I am one to begin this foolishness—
Just to shake your hand

*

wandering in a
double curve

*

the seriousness
of pleasure

*

"life conceived as a kind
of listening"
                    —Pater

*

IN SERVICE

The airplane is what we think it is.

*

proportion competes with
                    immediacy

*

By a reminder
    I'll be there
jumping the door

                    *

            OTHERS

    like so many equally breathless
    the stripes that make this
    something discrete—strapped
    to the standing fragment of an
    older temple

                    *

    GI
    AN
    TT
    EA
    RS

                    *

CORN   superficial traffic

                    *

East Kent   where the sky
                     meets the sea

                    *

at both ends of what
was said earlier
the polar bear's coat catches
the green light

                    *

ADMITTEDLY
THE ELBOW HITS
THE OPEN DRAWER
AND WE HAVE THIS.

*

Between "and" and "again"
            such a hole!

*

a voice I come back to
and explain my turn

*

night pulls the stones
        shifts the particulars

            I am grounded in
                possibilities

*

The Proud Possessors

        1) irrational fantasies
        2) delicate enigmas
        3) shocking juxtapositions
        4) weird incongruities

*

(windbag)   jelly gems

*

"Art is where construction
        and composition coincide."
                —Leo Stein

                *

My heart is a
live foreign object
and it wants
to die

            *

    a unity suffering its inception

            *

Death x Murder / Induced traumatic insult

            *

    "Space is the creation
        of our ancestors"
                —Poincare

            *

Punjabi: "In the first place"

Bengali: (Sorting the dust to find rice)

                    1971

CRIME LINEN

cabby anterior finick
dependence blank
hemmed mix
intrinsic   predator cupola sum
dash and still gorge just is making
managed
moon who's none making
incipience it comma navigate
that all get ware to set over agile
patina distend
streets

ram label hunch cart
grate snap poster hesitant heuristic
bush clock
deft announce row halter cave
gear walk
polythene pneumatic carbon luxe
sail   ward
lays crick
talon arbor loam week divest
Madison weir stew posit

sequel   vein
loaf   dug
        nail
raining loose
                    fibre
brink
arch air women   cafe   method
gram broom night hat
friends gate maneuver grasses   orb
fit lore
                orphan

        soil bar
mack fee
            numb
      lit
            crack torch

vast
              spinal
keel shock

dough   tag

gear
frank

inert

mercy flesh fruit on skull
murmur

telephone married early neon
householding

mice incense prosecutor reading
generator

fault observe general putty back
gnome

record Cherry floorboards Rajah
parson

mitten poll radio ermine sand
going

old frere border court home ail
thirds

reaches marks lamb rule hover creak
gnomon

fatal over no port guild stick
reflect

monumental
            diaphanous

                shoe
took rain

guise will   mare

salve cordon
lack
                raised

meadow

curtailment
ash medium

        both

speech mile
libertine

        ring

trajectory
reappear

        shadowy

dense fore
pyramiding

        flare

        shod

shaft
        ploy
gram
        ends

cracked zinnia

apprentice

gouache

gravel curt

mitten sixth

grate
        C & X

notion
        paste

emblem
        crisp

TUESDAY

She was clothes

She was narration

She was million

She was lakes and she was

She was forge

She was lopped off in charge of

She was fingers and telephoned

She was remembered for talking

She was forgotten again and again

She was knots

She was perhaps looked after

She was taken here and there

She was left behind and looked up

She was among some objects

She was a noun and a pronoun at last

She was walking

She was laughing

She was phrased if an island

She was complicating a number and other things

She was spelled

She was sought doves awkward

She was or do you know

She was changed by psychology

She was paid

She was the question

She was the vaseline

She was the sound of difference

She was the look of plural

She was regret insinuation but that

She was attention meant

She was careful

She was always rather

She was overheard always rather

She was the reason

She was that are not

She was that are not as a result

She was level

She was doing anything leaves grass hoe

She was the pose

She was the pose a few years later

She was custom color how to among others

She was idle gospel

She was to go back

She was there when you saw her

She was she was

She was she wasn't

She was a mad clock

She was adamant

She was the reinstatement of bewilderment

She was there to preside

She was no tirade or newspaper

She was punctuated by piracy

She was relaxed water

1972

THE POLE IS THE ONE
PLACE ON EARTH THAT
DOESN'T TURN

I had my drink and we stepped out onto the terrace to look over the city.

"Modern man lives in an increasingly geometric order."

I told him I'd never heard of that before.

He paid the man and hoisted the crate up onto his shoulder and carried it back to the car. Then he led me to this particular cafe he seemed to know about.

I had my drink and we stepped out onto the terrace to look over the city.

"Modern man lives in an increasingly geometric order."

I paid the man and hoisted the crate up onto his shoulder and he carried it back to the car. I had my drink and we stepped out onto the terrace to look over the city. The blue water of the Pacific shimmered in the moonlight about a mile away. Just then a boy below us said something in Spanish that I didn't quite understand. I yelled back and the boy disappeared. Down in the port the fishing boats were casting their moorings; a sound of cars came from the highway and lights began to appear at the windows of the houses. The mist was getting heavier.

"If you study the cross-section of a steamship, your failure to consider the hold apart from the hurricane will result in a feeling of incipient insanity; you will begin to reel along the alley-ways. Ignorance, in such cases, is perhaps health, but it's a real shame."

I told him I'd never heard of that before.

He paid the man and hoisted the crate up onto his shoulder and carried it back to the car. I paid the waiter and staggered out after them. They drove so far out of town that I didn't know where I was. All I could see were the big hills in front of us.

The blue water of the Pacific shimmered in the bright light about a mile away. No one seemed very concerned.

"Is that you, dear Cousin, or your ghost?" I yelled back and the boy disappeared. All I could see were the big hills in front of us.

Towards noon the police arrived. They looked at our identity cards, and asked a few questions.

"Those pigs, they don't eat garbage?"

"I've never seen bigger ones."

"They live in houses like people?"

"Until now those pigs never knew what dirt was."

They told me they'd never heard of that before.

The blue water of the Pacific shimmered in the sunlight about a mile away. Down in the port the fishing boats were casting their moorings; a sound of cars came from the highway. No one seemed very concerned. All I could see were the big hills in front of us.

"Is that you, dear Cousin, or your ghost?"

With these words he seized his masked accuser and whirled into a hectic waltz, the others following his example, while their voices, with extraordinary versatility, mimicked violins, basses, oboes and French horns.

I paid the waiter and staggered out after them. All I could see were the big hills in front of us. Just then a boy said something in Spanish that I didn't quite understand. I yelled back and the boy disappeared.

The mist was getting heavier.

Down in the port the fishing boats were casting their moorings; a sound of cars came from the highway and lights began to appear at the windows of the houses. No one seemed very concerned.

FIVE

TWO TWISTED WIRES SPINNING

Merrill comes. Poems from Malanga come. Merrill tells me Kerouac died of a stroke 3 days ago in Florida. A letter from Slater comes asking for old poems he sent to me in Europe. Another new anthology comes. Betsi comes. Backache. A letter from Pepper Peddie comes asking for poems for SILO. The first issue of FIELD comes. A letter from Darrell comes. He is not in Albuquerque. Merrill tells me Ted is living in a room in Ann Arbor. Merrill comes into the kitchen and says Joyce never drank red wine because it reminded him of raw beefsteak. A letter from John Martin comes with Ed Dorn's address in England. A letter from Ann comes with a picture of me on Skiathos. Merrill and Betsi drink red wine. We eat pork chops, corn and mushrooms. I write: *Merrill tells me Ted is living.* Betsi goes into the kitchen. I write: *a letter from Ann comes with a picture of me on Skiathos.* Betsi goes to the Art Dept. Merrill goes to Mt. Gilead. I go to sleep. Backache.

10/69

IDIOM FEEL JOB

        sit down on your chair. not for good
will but for concrete goals. eyes solarized. critics
and man both. stimuli. the transfer takes place.
are you getting the guide? evening concerts? at-
tending harvard? electronically controlled bombs
are the total effect of bad advice. you telling me?
we're coming out of the woods mopping our
beards. tyrone sniper sleeps in the teamster hut.
16 degrees the hockey 18 minutes the huddles 33
seconds the toast. we go by. ugly wink. but for a
9th straight triumph. buy a magazine. shoot change
the retrospect. ah. to have you call it fool with the
horns. it'd be a pleasure like forever. other eye thin-
king up things to do with the weather. no plans no
complaints just the air door cloud convenience im-
patient energy can make the most of. he has water-
melon. we go by. the bone become the favorite means
of travel. dog in the mirror the candle arcs close to
skinny sleep. in sky out. blood in the tooth. hat in
hand. noise teaser rain shrink. a flat sun full of
echoes. my own one was simple. flew. i turned to
the patient door from my chair. i turned on the door
like a fat wolf and the parallels spoke english.

LONDON DAYS

        While she was in Brighton I was left
to look after the house in Kensington. Alone in
a 30 room Victorian mansion I began adapting
a story around some letters I found in a biscuit
tin under my bed. Unless it was raining I spent
my afternoons near the Round Pond in Kensing-
ton Gardens waiting for yesterday to catch up.

WITH THE DOG CAME THE LETTERS

A few chuckles from the station attendant, "You folks going up there tonight?" A plane was approaching. "Old Mrs Nouvelle's been dead for some time." The plane passed over and into the twilight. Jack started the car and the attendant grinned. "Nobody living up there now. You sure you got the right address?" Lana was still asleep on the back seat as we approached the Nouvelle house. Jack reached across the front seat and took the revolver from my purse. "Just in case." I switched on the radio. Lana stirred and whimpered. "You're not afraid are you?" I looked away. "Of course I am." "Maybe you should stay here with Lana." Another car was coming up the driveway with its lights off. "Turn off the radio. That's probably Nova and Bryher." The car pulled up about 100 yards behind us and flashed its lights 3 times. Jack got out and started down the driveway toward their car. Two shots rang out. I switched on the radio again. Lana was still sleeping.

ACE OF LIES

for Tom

                        supreme delicacy filling the grey
afternoon dreaming its blessed delay rolling a counterfeit
cloud through the room recommending itself to the conversation

        and what he admired and what he admired most was the
violin taking him through all the foolishness taking him
with its resigned melancholy through the reaches of his thoughts
in laughter

           that seemed enough

                    more than enough to ask

to be taken

         taken

            what he admired most

congeal

      laugh

        hand over

                    the betting fully

understood

composure's longshot nostalgia

5/72

DOGS WINDOW

Zinn: Head down I must translate
The work and worry.
Who can write the long sentence?
Who can't?
Who can endure it?

Maaf: Impartial from the room,
Forehead to the sky
I stroll the white lawn.
Never a night sky.
Never an empty street.

Zinn: Classic parody, witty negation.
What's there to want?
Mid-progress built in.
O my chest is full
Of hesitation!

Maaf: I have drawn a line
To last season's window.
I don't look for the sun.
I don't care to see the cars.
It's the path alone appeals.
I can hear it. Working souvenir.

Zinn: Canny judgements notice me.
My need's through with its energies.
Am I done for?
How the future cuts me with its logic!
Can I be asleep? Masterful?

Maaf: I listen and eternity feints.
Shame could be a friend now
In what seems the season for it.
Daggers broken. Blood caresses us.
The less whimsical beard reasons
I guess.

Zinn: Half know their idyll.
       Found soon enough.
       But I am here with my
       Green ink for harking back.

Maaf: Walking out on memories
       For a sleep. Warm stone
       Follows the profile.
       Brighter accident!
       Give the man a cigar!
       No one ever said that to me.

Zinn: Who liked the laugh?
       Who likes the laugh
       Shoots the lion.
       Big brain! Interesting ideas
       Always seem the same.

Maaf: Zinn Zinn Zinn Zinn!
       It's volume stops this tune!
       Stops it with a stab
       In the spectre's back.

Zinn: The work and worry
       Instead of the brick and song
       Eh?

Maaf: Instead of.

By Ray DiPalma

MAX
MACAROONS (with Stephen Shrader)
BETWEEN THE SHAPES
CLINCHES
THE GALLERY GOERS
ALL BOWED DOWN
WORKS IN A DRAWER
BORGIA CIRCLES
TIME BEING (with Asa Benveniste & Tom Raworth)
SOLI